How to Analyze People

————— ❧❧❧❧ —————

A Beginner's Guide to Analyzing, Understanding, and Predicting People's Behavior

Jessica Greiner

purposes and should thus be thought of as universal. As befitting its nature, it is presented without assurance regarding its prolonged validity or interim quality. Trademarks that are mentioned are done without written consent and can in no way be considered an endorsement from the trademark holder.

This book is designed to provide accurate and authoritative information in regard to the subject matter covered. By its sale, neither the publisher nor the author is engaged in rendering psychological or other professional services. If expert assistance or counseling is needed, the services of a competent professional should be sought.

Table of Contents

Introduction

Congratulations and thank you for choosing How to Analyze People: A Beginner's Guide to Analyzing, Understanding, and Predicting People's Behavior.

Many sayings show how much we reflect on human behavior. "You can never understand a man until you've walked a mile in his shoes," "What you see is what you get," "Never judge a book by its cover." All of these expressions show that how we interact with people is a matter of great concern for most of us. If you take the time to analyze them, you'll see there is at least a small kernel of truth that applies to all of us.

Even though we can hear about a man's experience, it doesn't mean we truly understand how he feels. It is almost impossible to show empathy when someone talks about the breakup of their family if we have never gone through it ourselves. We don't really know what is on the inside of a person until we can dig a little deeper below the surface and draw it out.

But even though these expressions are very common, one of them seems to be lacking in truth. We often hear people make the statement: "What you see is what you get." While this may be the case with some people, the reality is very few people really show their true character when around others. In fact, you might find that you can live in the same household with someone, share the same experiences, and believe the same things yet still come out feeling like you don't know them.

There is a good reason why this happens. If you understand even the slightest bit about human interactions, you already know that people are rarely willing to reveal they're true selves. It is a natural tendency to want to protect themselves in a positive light. That's why many go to such lengths to hide any imperfections, flaws, or otherwise negative qualities from outsiders. It is only after we've known someone for a period, built up some relationship with them, and have come to believe on some level that they can be trusted to keep our secrets that we will finally let our guard down just a little bit. But even still, it is very rare that someone knows everything there is to know about another person.

Most people tend to keep their true selves hidden underneath many layers of masks and project outward someone other than who they are meant to be. This is a common occurrence among people regardless of their background, culture, or genetics. It is basically referred to as the Social Penetration Theory (or the onion theory), and it can explain exactly why we often have difficulty understanding the other people we interact with.

Communication is not about words as some people may believe. It's about peeling away the many different layers of a personality. These layers are usually displayed to us in their behavior, mannerisms, physical gestures, and even their tone of voice. We all understand this concept when it applies to us, but we struggle to grasp hidden meanings when we are dealing with others.

Social Penetration points out that we only reveal our innermost layers after our relationships have reached a certain depth. For example, initially when we first meet someone, our defenses are high, so we only disclose superficial information. We may only reveal facts and details about ourselves that won't bounce back and cause us harm or be used against us. As the relationship continues to grow, we gradually reveal more information about ourselves. We begin to lower our guard and are more likely to reveal more intimate details increasingly with the right person. It is as if we are peeling back layers over time until the person we are interacting with is brought into our innermost circle.

This is how we build relationships with one another. The more personal the facts we share with each other, the closer the bond becomes. Your ability to see through those layers is directly connected with your ability to read people. But that is only the beginning. It will also be important for you to be able to understand yourself.

It can be surprising to know just how many people truly do not understand their characteristics and emotional or mental makeup. But if you want to learn how to read people, it is important that you do so.

Each one of us is basically made up of genetics, past experiences, and responses to our cultural influences. We may not realize it, but much of our opinions about others are based on this mixed pot of life. And if we're not careful, we can put up a host of mental barriers that can prevent us from seeing past the many layers of the people around us to get to the real person that lies underneath. So, one of the first things you'll need to do before you can successfully begin to read people is to unlearn the many biases, prejudices, and other opinions you've developed and then wipe the slate clean.

Learning to break through these mental barriers is not always easy. Yes, there are those that are easily identifiable, but the hardest ones to get rid of are those we're not even aware of. They may be the result of hidden fears from past experiences we don't even remember. They could be from untruths we've heard in the past, or they could be rooted in base teachings and preconditioning you've had since youth. Whatever the source is, you need to start rooting them out, and once you do, you'll find that your eyes will be opened and you'll start to see things unfolding right in front of them.

Through the pages of this book, be prepared to learn just as much about yourself as you do about other people. We are naturally inquisitive people, and we want to know everything we can about the world around us, especially about those who we interact with daily. You'll discover that at the very heart of your fears lies your own inability to read people. With that in mind, you can expect to understand:

- Basic aspects of human behavior

- How you can become a better communicator

- How the brain and behavior are connected

- How to read between the lines and uncover the truth

- What the body is really saying, how to read actions, not words

- Different personality types and how to interact with them

- And how to uncover what's not being said in any given situation

We hope that the book will reveal valuable information that will allow you to discover a better way to interact with all the different types of people in your life.

There are plenty of books on this subject on the market, so thanks again for choosing this one! Every effort was made to ensure it is full of as much useful information as possible; please enjoy!

Chapter 1:

The Brain and Behavior

It's no wonder that many people have difficulty communicating and understanding each other. We don't really know what's going on inside the minds of other people. We are often led to believe that everything we see is all we need to communicate but there is so much more to it.

If you were lucky enough to grow up in the '60s or '70s, then you're probably familiar with a well known comic by the name of Flip Wilson. Flip had a punchline that everyone could relate to. No matter what offensive thing he did, he could always excuse it away with the one line. "The devil made me do it." While most of us found his line humorous, it reveals a great deal about the human psyche. We all do it at one time or another. It is easy for us to pass responsibility on to someone else. Flip often blamed the invisible devil for his shenanigans but who do we blame? Definitely not ourselves, it is so much easier to pass the consequences on to another party.

The truth is, we often see in other people the very actions we know we are guilty of. We find that if something happens, someone says or does something we don't like, this is usually the first thing we want to point out to the other person. It is the very thing that we are afraid of finding in ourselves. Sadly, many of us can readily see these negative aspects in other people but never in ourselves. The reality is the ability to get along with others really lies within ourselves. The things we find offensive in many people are usually their ideas, beliefs, and opinions that we have already formed and unconsciously judged them for.

So, rather than blame Flip Wilson's "devil" for his wayward actions, we could change his line and coin a completely new phrase. "My brain made me do it."

The Basics

Because of what happens in our unconscious mind, we have mastered the ability to manipulate our view of the world in a way that is more pleasing to us. When we face an uncomfortable situation, we automatically begin to create a mental environment that makes us feel more comfortable.

When our unconscious mind is at work, it often looks for the easy way out of a situation. It excuses our behavior while continuously pointing the finger at everyone else around us. Whether we want to label it curiosity, jealousy, or individualism, our inner mind is always looking for an excuse for our actions.

This kind of mental self-defense is called projection. It is a way to provide relief from the anxiety we feel about a certain situation. The problem is that the relief we get from this "blame the other guy" concept is that it doesn't last long. We can only fool ourselves for a very short period. Like a ricochet bullet, it will bounce off of wherever it aims and eventually, it will come back to us. This adds even more stress and anxiety to our lives, and we end up looking suspiciously at everyone else rather than addressing the negativity that is within us—that nagging feeling that is always behind how we view other people.

What's Really Causing Your Behavior

Science has come a long way in helping us understand the power of the human brain and how it works. Research has shown that the brain's frontal lobe is at the heart of our behavior and how we develop opinions about others. Science has come to understand that this area of the brain.

- Is where logical thinking takes place

- Gives us the power of self-control (or lack thereof)

- Is responsible for our moods and overall mental state of mind

- Lesions or any damage to the frontal lobe can influence our impulse reactions and behaviors

As more studies are completed, more information about the brain is revealed helping us to understand the mental gymnastics that are involved when we interact with other people. Even if we set aside cases of mental disorders or brain damage, this is where much of our own biases come from. Yes, we can excuse much of it based on influences by our upbringing, culture, and overall life experiences, but all of those things must be filtered through the frontal lobe of the brain before an opinion is formed.

Neurotransmitters

All of this starts to happen because of the neurotransmitters at work in the brain. These naturally occurring chemicals are triggered and released in response to certain situations and—when activated—are the beginning of an impulse that passes from one nerve cell to another. The axon of one nerve cell and the dendrites of another nerve cell cannot actually come in contact with each other. There is always a gap (called the synapse) that a message must pass through. It is the neurotransmitters that ensure that the messages get passed through.

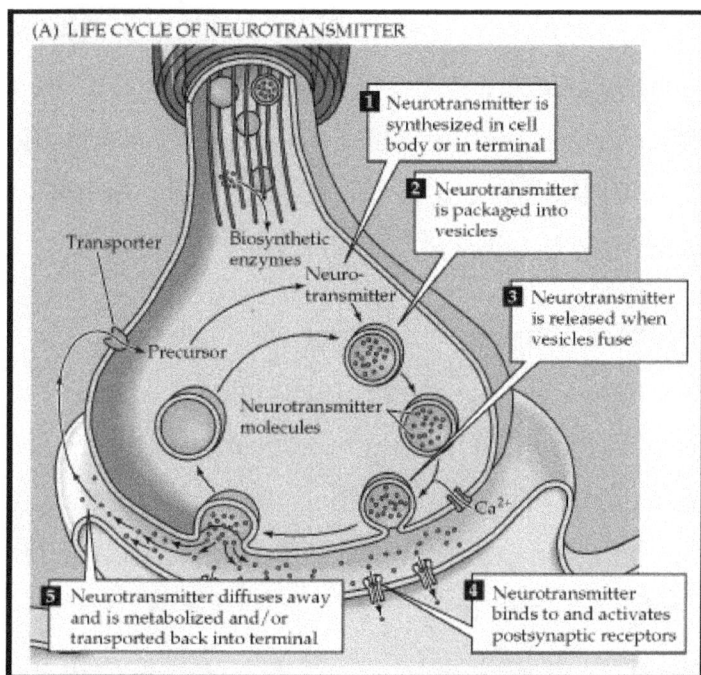

(A) LIFE CYCLE OF NEUROTRANSMITTER

Source: Life Cycle of Neurotransmitter [ONLINE]. Available at: http://www.wikipremed.com/mcat_course_psychology.php?module=1§i on=6 [Accessed 11 April 2018].

There are at least 50 different types of neurotransmitters found in the brain. Of these, acetylcholine and adrenaline are considered the most excitatory and others such as dopamine and serotonin are found at the opposite end of the spectrum and are the most inhibitory. Every neurotransmitter has a job to perform that involves regulating the activities of its specific area of the brain and are key elements in how a person is to behave.

In fact, nearly all behavioral patterns are regulated by this interconnecting process of the human brain. When these neurotransmitters are released, certain activities will automatically happen in the body. To get a better understanding of how this works, let's look at a diagram of human behavior as it develops in the brain.

Acetylcholine

Acetylcholine is the neurotransmitter that controls voluntary movement. It is also responsible for managing your memory, your ability to learn, and your sleeping patterns. Whenever someone has too much acetylcholine in their system, it can lead to depression and, in some extreme cases, dementia, and then when there is too few, a person may experience painful cramps throughout the body.

Serotonin

The neurotransmitter serotonin is responsible for regulating a person's inner drive. This can affect anything from their appetite and sex drive to their impulsive and aggressive behavior. When there is not enough serotonin, depression can set in along with a host of anxiety disorders.

Dopamine

A lack of dopamine can cause a person to lose the ability to concentrate, focus, or coordinate movements and too much of it can result in severe psychological disorders like schizophrenia.

Norepinephrine

Controls the glucose metabolism and the amount of energy the body consumes. When there is not enough of it, depression develops, and it can affect the muscles and heart rate. Sometimes referred to as adrenaline, it can also increase stress levels in the body.

Gamma-Amino Butyric Acid (GABA)

This is an inhibitor that can lower the level of excitability, and because of its effect on the brain's hippocampus, it can help with learning and memory. Too much and it can easily trigger anxiety disorders.

Endorphins

Endorphins are often released in painful or stressful situations. It can also contribute feelings of pleasure. It is often a key element to lowering pain in many situations.

Chapter 1: The Brain and Behavior

Understanding how neurotransmitters can impact a person's behavior and can be one of the key components of being able to read people successfully. Since the chemistry of the brain directs much of our activities, whether voluntary in involuntary, understanding this can help us understand the other people we interact with.

It won't matter much if you can see that someone is extremely angry if their brain chemistry is overloaded with the wrong type of neurotransmitter. Of course, these are not the only factors in understanding human behavior but they can be a key element in what is driving a person to a specific type of behavior and can help to explain why certain patterns are evident in their actions.

The Power of Intuition

Many people question whether or not intuition is a real thing. They often point out that what we think is intuition is simply a rational person who is conscious of his environment and the impact it has on his surroundings. However, after extensive research, we have come to understand that decisions based on intuition are often performed in areas of the brain that are not key components of our language or reasoning ability. When it comes to intuition, decisions and actions are often performed without any logical reasoning or thought process but rather on a "gut feeling" they may have about a certain environment.

But what exactly is intuition and why should we care about it? The dictionary defines it as the instant ability to understand a situation without having to reason on it. In essence, it is an inherent awareness of something that influences us internally. Basically, we know something that we should not know.

How does the brain work with intuition?

When we make a decision, many areas of the brain are activated. Each one is seeking to influence the other parts of the brain so there are lots of signals firing, targeting the primary area where the decisions will be made. We might assume that this is a matter of free will, but there is actually a voting process going on where each area involved in the decision gets a vote. The area of the brain with the most votes wins and the decision is made in their favor.

Each section of the brain is fighting to protect its interests and has a say. This could mean that your natural instincts to provide for your needs will have input along with preconceived ideas about a situation, reasoning, memory, and the body's motor skills will all contribute to the decision-making process.

Much of this is done consciously, but a great deal of this decision-making process happens in the unconscious mind. We know that our brain is working out a decision when you can literally hear yourself think. This is a conscious activity going on in the brain, but there are other aspects of the process that we may not be aware of. This process triggers a "feeling" that is unexplainable—this is intuition at work.

We find ourselves aware of something that we don't really know how we know it. Intuition is often at the base of many of our fears. This is a genetically programmed part of our instincts. Think of it as you would think of bears sleeping through the winter or birds flying south. Once certain situations present themselves, our internal system gives us a signal to stop or change our behavior. Intuition dictates our perception of a situation and our physiology by raising our blood pressure and preparing us to take whatever action is necessary for the moment.

We rely heavily on our intuition to help us to sense danger by causing our intestines to contract. This is where the idea of the gut feeling comes from. The senses in the gut let us know of a possible threat and dictates what behavior happens after that.

All of this happens in our unconscious mind. For thousands of years, this feeling has helped many to survive all sorts of situations. The fight or flight response is not the result of reasoning and logic, but that of intuition—that inner voice that dictates our actions in any given set of circumstances. However, it is also a key component in people's behavior in today's modern world. With the rate of new developments coming at us in rapid succession, our instincts can dictate what we do in all sorts of situations. From navigating heavy traffic to how we interact with people, intuition may be a major factor that needs to be considered when we read people.

You can have people from a wide variety of backgrounds with different levels of intuition. You will find some who rely almost entirely on their gut instincts, but you will also find those who ignore that inner impulse completely, making every choice strictly by the book. Ideally, the best people to interact with are those who have a healthy balance that follows basic rules and guidelines but keeps them tempered with that gut feeling that helps them to be wary of possible dangers.

The bottom line is by understanding how the brain and intuition work, we can begin to perceive not just that people are making certain choices but why they may be responding to a specific situation. The more capable you are at understanding the underlying impulses to their actions the easier it will be to read people and interact positively with them.

Chapter 2:
Advantages of Being Able
to Read People

The masses often ridicule people who are effective at analyzing their environment. We live in a world where scrutiny is often discouraged. As we experience a life full of advanced technology, there is a new dividing line that is beginning to appear. Those who want to understand the world they live in and perhaps study things a bit more closely, and those that simply want to follow the masses without putting much thought into it.

The fact that you're reading this book is an indication that you are a part of the more analytical side of things. However, rather than be discouraged by all of those people who are less inclined to see the point in your need to understand the people around you, you can be confident that there are many good reasons to learn how to read people. The advantages will definitely put you ahead of many others in many areas of life.

Makes You a Better Communicator

Once you are better able to read people, you'll find that others will be more inclined to come to you for advice when they have to interact with others. You might find yourself being asked to break down different messages or actions they have received or to brainstorm certain problems or challenges they have with the different people they interact with.

You'll become a natural problem solver, and your employers and coworkers will likely gravitate to you as a mediator in issues of conflict resolution. The more you can understand people, the more

you'll be able to show empathy, which will
naturally make you a better friend and a better
confidant in both your personal and professional
life.

As you come to understand many of the things
you will learn in this book, you'll start to analyze
everything around you in excruciating detail.
You'll see things you never noticed before, and
your perspective in life will begin to change.
You'll teach your brain how to look at events
from an entirely different point of view giving
you more insight than you ever had before.

Makes You More Empathetic

Another natural advantage of learning to read
people is your ability to be more tolerant of other
people's differences. Rather than expecting
everyone to see things the way you see the world,
you will learn that not everything is always

written in black and white and that there are flaws in every perspective.

This understanding will make you more compassionate and considerate of other people's feelings, and you will become kinder and be willing to show more feeling. Along with that comes a greater sense of responsibility. Once you understand how your actions can affect other people, you will be more conscientious about things you do that could hurt their feelings, disappoint them, or discourage them.

A good example of this is developing a deeper respect for other people's time. People who are often late for meetings or social gatherings are an irritation to those who are more time-conscious. When you realize the efforts that people put in to make sure that a meeting is planned carefully, your promises will make you more reliable and willing to stick with your commitments.

You'll Feel Smarter

Your new perception of the world will make you feel smarter. The exercises you apply in this book will naturally stretch your brain's ability to see things. You'll be more in tune with the minutia of things going on around you, and you'll pick up on all sorts of small details that you would never have noticed before. In time, you'll become more knowledgeable about all sorts of things, which will make you more efficient in your own responsibilities as well as knowledgeable in conversations you have with all sorts of things. You'll become an astute conversationalist, able to discuss all manner of topics in detail.

Improved Ability to Sum Up Situations

Regardless of the situation, you'll be able to see through much of the quagmire that most people get caught up with. Preparation for events will be easier, and you'll quickly know your place in any given situation. Because those who are able to read people have very active minds, you'll always be on and prepared to engage in a meaningful conversation, know how to debate an issue and engage in interactions that are stimulating for other people.

Despite these advantages, those who read people can peel back the many layers of hidden truths that people try to keep out of sight. If you're not careful, eventually all of this can be overwhelming as we learn so much about other people. We'll be on a continuous treadmill to improve ourselves and end up over-analyzing many situations.

Chapter 2: Advantages of Being Able to Read People

The secret, therefore, is to find a happy balance. The truth is that there is no end to the secrets you'll be able to uncover so you'll have to find that happy medium when you can say I know enough and choose not to dig any deeper for the countless hidden secrets in the lives of so many people. If you can do this, you'll be a much happier and more productive person for doing so.

Chapter 3:
What You Didn't Know About Behavior (What You See Every Day)

It is said that communication is only 20% words and another 80% body language. If that's the case, it helps to understand the fundamentals of human physiology. We need to know what physical actions, movements, and expressions people make that reveal their true inner feelings. In short, you need a basic course in psychology.

This does not have to be an extremely complicated lesson dealing with detailed and complicated textbooks that explain the human mind. It can be just a basic and general understanding of the other 80% of communication that all people do. We've already discussed the importance of neurotransmitters and intuition in controlling our behavior, but now we're going to look at the seeds of motivation, emotions, understanding, and communication.

If after reading this book, you're interested in delving deeper into the subject, there are numerous programs online that will allow you to gather research materials from reports on clinical trials and experiments. But as the average person who is not seeking this as a career move, the basic understanding of the fundamentals of human interaction should be sufficient.

When it comes to analyzing people, people communicate in three basic ways and being able to recognize these cues is key to successfully determining what people are really saying. They communicate through facial expressions, through body language, and through human psychology. Each one of these is a component of human physiology and can be used in a myriad of ways, and many are done without the user actually realizing what he's really doing.

You not only need to understand how these things are used but also to what degree the message is being sent. While everyone uses these three elements, they do not all use them to the same degree. There are definitely variations in use that you'll have to determine. The best way to do this is by spending time with the other individual. In time, by observing their mannerisms, you will be able to determine to what degree they are communicating with you. We will discuss each of these methods in more detail later in the book but for now, let's just get a general overview of how these tools are used in communication.

Facial Profiling

If you're one of those people who does not enjoy talking on the phone, it is probably because you have become accustomed to facial profiling without even realizing it. Our face is much like a blank canvas and can reveal a great deal about what we are thinking, believe, and feel. It is probably the most visible reflection of the inner you that exists.

The face can help you understand what is not being spoken and the inner characteristics of the people we interact with. Learning how to read faces have been around for centuries, and even today countless research studies are going on that give evidence that your face reveals much about the inner person within, to a much greater extent than the words you speak. In general, there are five different types of facial expressions you will encounter. Each one will tell you a great deal about the person you are trying to read. Identifying each type of facial expression deals more with the physical features of the face than the message the person is sending.

Convex

© Buzzle.com

Convex: Those with convex facial expressions usually have a prominent forehead, especially around the brows where it slopes backward as it rises. Their eyes are quite full with a long nose that is high in the bridge area. They have a strong mouth, and their lips are pushed out with a receding chin.

People with a convex face have been known to be relatively stubborn and demanding, showing very little patience when dealing with other people. They are quick thinkers and make good business partners as they have a strong affinity for those skills that are best needed in business.

Concave

© Buzzle.com

Concave: The concave face is characterized by a strong and prominent chin and a protruding forehead that is flat above the brows. They have small noses and deep-set eyes. Their mouth recedes, and their nose is large but slightly curved.

These people are considered to be good-natured and very patient. Their natural personality tends to be to take things slow and make deliberate actions. They are more meditative and can endure a lot. Their interests usually lie in philosophies and theories. However, they tend to be more absent-minded than others, but they are determined and dependable, making every move they make deliberate.

Plane

© Buzzle.com

Plane: Those with a plane face type generally have a perfectly balanced face. It is neither overdeveloped in any area nor is it underdeveloped. These people are considered to be very mild and stable. They are known for their consistent character and more balanced mental state.

Convex-Concave

© Buzzle.com

Convex-Concave: These faces have concave upper features while the lower features are convex. These people tend to have a very weak personality and are often very impulsive. Their personality tends to be unreliable and inconsistent.

Concave-Convex: This face type is the opposite of the Convex/Concave where the upper facial features are convex with a more noticeable and prominent forehead but a very weak chin characterizes the lower features. Moral weakness and emotional instability mainly identify this personality type.

Concave-
Convex
© Buzzle.com

However, they do have the capacity to show understanding and empathy with the people with whom they are closely associated.

Of course, it is not always as black and white as this. There are variations of these facial structures, and there are other factors that are also involved in determining personality types. For example, because women's features are not as sharp as men, it is not always easy to distinguish which facial profile they have. Men, on the other hand, generally have sharper features and their profiles are much more easily distinguished, their facial personality is more readily identified.

Facial profiling is probably one of the first things you learn when you're trying to read people. By being able to identify these characteristics, you can already begin to formulate an idea of the person's personality and character even before the first word is spoken. With regular practice, you'll begin to notice and sum up a person in an instant.

Beyond this, other types of facial profiling can enhance the basics of the personality types. Rather than looking at the profile of a person, you can also look at the shape of their faces.

Round: People who have round faces tend to have faces that are a little fat around the cheeks.

They are usually known to be emotional and very sensitive. Because of this, they tend to be more stable in a relationship.

Oblong: Oblong faces are long and very thin. People with this shape tend to be more athletic and have a more muscular physique. These people generally are very methodical and practical when working and have a very narcissistic demeanor, which can cause problems in relationships.

Square: People with square faces usually have higher analytical skills and are considered to be very intelligent. They can be very decisive but also can be quite dominating and aggressive.

Triangular: A person with a thin body and a triangular face is often believed to be highly intellectual. These people usually tend to have a fiery temper but are also very creative.

Chapter 3: What You Didn't Know About Behavior (What You See Every Day)

We all know and understand that our personality is defined by our DNA and is something that is unique to each one of us. However, the theory that just as the DNA determines our physical features by giving us a round face, long nose, or deep-set eyes, those physical features are directly connected to our internal personality.

Some may question whether this type of facial profiling can be really accurate because it generalizes large groups of people and clumps them all together. However, there does seem to be scientific evidence to its accuracy. Faception, a company founded in 2014 has had a great deal of success in identifying potential terrorists and other criminal types simply by analyzing faces in a crowd.

The theory behind this idea is not new and has been around for thousands of years. It is only recently, though, that the science behind it has evolved to the level it is today. According to scientific research, our personalities are affected by our genetics, and our face is simply a physical representation of our DNA.

It is important to know that facial mapping is not as basic as it might first appear. There are, of course, many other factors that are also measured in facial profiling. However, when done correctly, with the proper skills and knowledge, companies like Faception can work with the leading homeland security agencies in different countries to provide an added layer of security in their countries as well supporting other businesses in determining whether a person is trustworthy or not.

Micro-Expressions

Another means of analyzing the face is through micro-expressions. As the saying goes, *"The face is the window to the soul."* However, to look out that window, you must first know how to read it. We just talked about how to identify different personality types by their facial features. We can now take this facial analysis to another level.

One of the first things you need to know is how to identify and correctly interpret these small and barely noticeable facial expressions.

What is a Micro-Expression: A micro-expression is a tiny, involuntary facial expression that reflects the inner emotions that a person is experiencing at the moment. It is different from regular pro-longed expressions that are made consciously. Because they are involuntary, it is very difficult to fake a micro-expression.

There are seven different types of micro-expressions, and they are the same on every person regardless of their culture, age, background, or any other factor. These expressions usually occur within 1/15 to 1/25 of a second after being triggered, so they happen very quickly.

While the face is the best place to read someone's emotions, it is often the one place that is overlooked. However, according to research, we have learned that these micro-expressions are universal. In essence, the expression used for happiness in the African Congo is the same expression used for happiness in the Alaskan Tundra. This is not a feature that is used by a unique group of people. It is not visually based. Studies have also shown that people who have been blind from birth and have never seen a micro-expression in their lives also make these same expressions.

This means that these expressions are part of our genetic makeup. We can't hide from them nor can we ever stop making them. So, to be able to read people, you need to know what to look for because no matter what situation you are in, these expressions will be evident.

Surprise:

- The eyebrows are raised and arched.
- The skin underneath is stretched tight.
- Horizontal wrinkles stretch across the forehead.
- Eyelids are open wide with the whites showing both and above and below the pupils.
- The jaw drops open, and the upper and lower teeth are parted but without any tension in the mouth.

Fear

- The eyebrows a raised but are pulled together making a flat line.
- Wrinkles form in the middle of the forehead between the eyebrows.

- The upper eyelid is raised, but the lower eyelid is tensed and tight.
- The white above the pupil can be seen but not the white below.
- The mouth is open, but the lips are stretched and drawn tightly back.

Disgust:

- Both the upper and lower eyelids are raised.
- The nose is wrinkled.
- The cheeks are pulled tight.
- Lines can be seen below the lower eyelid.
- The upper lip curls up into a snarl.
- The lower lip is tense and pulled tight.

This is the same expression you would make if you smelled something offensive.

Anger:

- The eyebrows are lowered and drawn tightly together.
- Vertical lines in the shape of the number 11 appear between the eyebrows.
- The lower lid is tense.
- The eyes make a hard stare or bulge out.
- Lips are pressed firmly together with the corners pointing downward or open in a square shape (like you are shouting).
- Nostrils are dilated.
- The lower jaw is pushed outward.

In this micro-expression, the entire face must be engaged. There should be no relaxation in any part of the face to show true anger.

Happiness:

- The corners of the lips are pulled back and upwards.

- The mouth could be open, and if so, the teeth are exposed.
- A wrinkle forms from the outer edge of the nose and runs down to the corner of the mouth.
- Cheeks are raised.
- There may be wrinkles formed on the lower eyelid.
- Crows feet appear at the outer edges of the eyes.

There is an intensity visible in this expression. It should be relatively easy to identify a fake expression by the degree of intensity of the facial features.

Sadness:

- The inside corners of the eyebrows are pulled in and up.

- The skin underneath the eyebrow forms a triangle with the inner corner pointing upward.
- The outside corners of the lips are pulled downward.
- The jaw is pulled upward.
- The lower lip pushes outward in a pout.

Contempt/Hate:

- Only one corner of the mouth is pulled up and back on one side.
- The eyes remain neutral.
- This is the only expression that forms on only one side of the face.
- It can vary in intensity. The depth of the emotion can vary. At its strongest, one eyebrow may lower.
- The lower eyelid can rise on the same side.

One of the most difficult challenges of reading these expressions is catching them when they appear. If the person you are trying to read wants to hide his emotions, they will last for only a fraction of a second. The best way to learn how to identify these feelings is to practice these expressions yourself while looking in the mirror. If you can readily detect and identify them in your own face, you'll be more likely to be able to identify them in someone else's.

Once you have mastered the ability to identify them in yourself, start looking for them in faces of people close to you. You already know their personality and their unique characteristics so it will be much easier for you to identify them first before you will see them in the faces of strangers.

Identifying micro-expressions is only one part of being able to read people successfully. Being able to read them gives you only a small glimpse into what is going on in the minds of people. Many other factors need to be taken into consideration. However, for those that can analyze their personality traits and their micro-expressions, you are well on your way to understanding them and what they are really trying to tell you.

Behavioral Patterns

In the beginning, identifying micro-expressions and facial styles may be a little difficult to do. Until you get the hang of it, another way to read people is by watching their behavioral patterns. For the layperson, this is probably the simplest way to determine what a person is really saying to you.

Think back to when you were a child, and your mother or father was upset with you. All you had to do was walk into the room where they were and in an instant, you knew something was wrong, They didn't say anything, it was that look, the way they stood, that tilt of the head or some other mannerism that told you that you were in big trouble.

Behavioral patterns are common to all of us. By understanding these silent messages, we can learn exactly what many find difficult to say with the spoken word. There are many different aspects of human nature, and these signals can often be missed, yet they are the key to helping us to become better communicators with everyone around us.

Most disagreements people have with one another start with a misunderstanding. Someone says something that gives the other party a false impression of a situation. They follow the course only to find later that they are doing something the other party never wanted. These false impressions can often lead us astray and can be a major cause of conflict, eventually alienating us all from one another.

This problem often evolves because we have failed to see the picture in its entirety or because we have not considered these non-verbal cues. Of course, knowing all of this information does not guarantee that it will eliminate conflict in your life, but it can certainly help reduce the number of issues you have.

We can rely on the hidden messages behind these behaviorisms because there is a reason why people make these gestures, take the body positions, and react to situations the way they do. Most people assume that these are just quirky mannerisms, but once you learn what someone is communicating towards you, it will be easier for you to know the best way to respond. The secret to understanding them is looking at them in reverse and tracing the behavior back to its origin.

This requires you to be able to look below the surface to find the tiny little nuances of meaning that every person has developed. It is a complex science, but as we go through this section, you'll learn at least the basics, and then if you wish, you can choose to study the matter even further. Just keep in mind that to understand all of these little details, it must begin with you and your perceptions of a particular situation.

You Don't Have All the Information

One of the reasons people have difficulty in understanding these behavioral patterns is because they don't have all the information to grasp the depth of a situation properly. Without some prior knowledge of the person, you are more likely to perceive an action by someone else based on your own past experiences. It could also be behavior that the person has carried over from an experience they had before coming into contact with you.

You've probably heard the story of the man whose boss yelled at him about his work. The man then goes home and yells at his wife, who then turns around and yells at the child, who turns around and kicks the dog. In each of these situations, the anger and frustration they felt had nothing to do with what was really going on, but they reacted negatively to an innocent party just the same.

In such cases, it may appear to be hostility directed at you, but in reality, it had absolutely nothing to do with you. This type of lashing out can come from a wide range of circumstances and can be the result of all types of emotions. It could be from grief over a loss; they may be suffering from physical or emotional pain, or in many cases, it could be a side effect of their medication. Whatever the case, it is very important first to learn what is behind someone's anger before you react to it.

Getting to the source of the anger may be all that is needed to diffuse a situation. However, without any knowledge of the person, it can be very difficult to read into the different behaviors of an individual. So, below are a few guidelines that can help you to learn how to read other people's behavior.

- **Start by getting to know the person**

  While all people display the same general mannerisms, they will show them in different degrees. Some will be more animated; others will be more subtle. Don't think of these behaviors in black and white terms. Instead, think of them as if they are on a spectrum with one end being those people who show extreme behavior and on the other end are those who are milder. All people will fall somewhere on this spectrum but not in the same way.

For this reason, it helps to have a baseline of their normal behavior before you can determine what they are really trying to say about you. A person who has ADHD may tap his feet constantly, and it could be easy to assume that they are bored or are irritated, but in reality, it just might be a nervous mannerism. So, it is important that you know a little bit about the person before you can be sure of what they really mean.

- **Look for deviations from their normal behavior**

Once you are familiar with their normal behavioral patterns, you will be able to see deviations more clearly. To a stranger, this may appear as a quirk, but you will know exactly what that scratching of the nose really means.

- **Look for several unusual behaviors**

  Generally, a single gesture or mannerism out of place may not mean much, but if you see them performing several unusual mannerisms together, then it is a pretty strong indication that something is not quite right. A person that is constantly clearing his throat may have a cough or a cold, but if you find he is also patting his feet, scratching his head and pacing the floor, it is a pretty clear indication that he is sending you a message.

- **Compare**

  If you notice any behavior that is out of character for the person, then you need to take your analysis a little further. Observe them see if they are displaying the same mannerisms with anyone else. Observe their interactions and watch their facial expressions to see if the issue is with you or they are sharing their feelings with others as well. It will give you valuable insight into what is really going on.

- **Check to see if they are mirroring you**

Humans tend to mirror other people. If you are nervous, you may be displaying your own mannerisms without even realizing it, and they may simply be mirroring your actions or that of someone else. In our nervous system, there are specific neurons that are designed to reflect back to someone else their own actions. For example, if you are happy to see someone, you will naturally smile when you see them, and they will automatically smile back. If they don't reflect your own emotions, then they are sending you a signal that they don't feel the same way.

- **Observe the walk**

You can tell a lot about a person by the way they walk. Under normal circumstances, people who walk swiftly and upright are often portrayed as a leader. It shows confidence and purpose. However, if a person meanders along, with his head bowed down low or shuffling his feet, it shows a lack of confidence and a lack of purpose.

Of course, this should be taken in context. For example, someone who is on vacation and strolling through the fashion district is not going to have the same sense of purpose as someone who is at work and on his way to a business meeting. Also, if there is an emergency of some kind you can fully expect some people to be walking with purpose. So, as you analyze this behavior, always measure it against the context of the present situation.

- **Listen for specific language**

While this section is about behavior, you can consider a person's choice of words as another aspect of their behavior. Not in the sense that they will speak exactly what's on their mind, but you should at least consider their choice of words in context. If they are using profanity or offensive language, it is sending a strong message, but even here there is room for several variables.

Words alone do not reveal the personal characteristics of an individual, but they can give you some insight into how they think. Their choice of adverbs and adjectives can tell you how they really feel about a situation. For example, if they make the statement "I went to the doctor today," it is simply a statement of fact, but if they enhance the sentence by saying "I rushed to the doctor today," it gives you a sense of urgency.

Bottom line, body language is a major part of communication and has been for many reasons. It is built into us for several reasons. If you're not entirely convinced, try this experiment. Ask someone to tell you their favorite story and then observe how they move their body as they relay the details of the story. Then after they finish, ask them to tell the story again but this time while sitting on their hands.

Right away, you'll notice that the animation in their voice, their level of enthusiasm, and their ability to remember the story lose its power. It is the same story, but it is nearly impossible to relate it in a way that reflects how they feel about it without using their body. This is a very complex form of communication, and we will discuss it in more detail in chapter five.

Human Nature

We also need to look at our own human nature. There are obvious elements of human nature that we can point to as a means of communicating. We talk, we interact, we are social beings, and we are inquisitive. These are all elements that are inbred in us from birth. But when it comes to communicating there is much more of our human nature involved in the process than we might think.

We all have our unique set of idiosyncrasies, quirks, and characteristics that set us apart from other creatures. We use these features to communicate with one another, and it is necessary to understand these things when we are trying to read people. There are in fact, several universal truths that are exclusive to being human that we need to understand.

- The scientific mind: As humans, we have a strong scientific mind. We are always trying to solve problems, categorize things, and predict how things work. While you may not be interested in science per se, the fact that you are reading this book shows you have a scientific mind. You want to analyze people so you can understand how to categorize them for future interactions. As such, people will often ask questions and seek answers, and in doing so may reflect certain traits that are unique to them.

- The need for fairness: No matter what society or culture you live in, there is an inherent need for fairness. This is why there is often a cry for justice when we sense there is no balance in our society. When a person perceives something as being unfair, they will react in different ways. Depending on the strength of their feeling about the situation, they may protest loudly, or they may launch a quiet protest. All of these actions are merely an attempt to fulfill that inner need for justice in their world.

- The need for privacy: Another part of human nature that can drastically affect our behavior is the need for privacy. This is why we often hibernate behind locked doors and keep secrets. No other creation on the planet is as concerned for privacy as the human. So if you notice that someone is becoming more standoffish, reluctant to be included in something public, analyze the situation and try to determine if they are simply attempting to protect their personal need for privacy.

Much of our behavioral patterns are directly related to our desire to fulfill an inner need that all humans share. While some people may not, on the surface, seem to care about these things. It is a part of our makeup no matter where we come from. Anyone who is attempting to learn how to analyze people will do well to try to grasp the full extent of how our own human nature affects the way we perceive the world around us and how we react to certain situations. By taking the time to look at a situation to determine what element of human nature the person is addressing, you may be surprised to find that there is a lot more about a person than what you may have originally thought.

Chapter 4:
Reading the Lie

It is said that you will be told at least three lies within every ten minutes of conversation. You may not realize it as your conversation seems to be flowing naturally and on a verbal level, everything seems to be right. However, according to statistics 91% of people regularly lie. If you're looking to become a human lie detector, you'll need to equip yourself with a good set of tools.

Once you learn how to identify lies when they are told, you'll also gain a nice little side effect. You'll be able to uncover hidden emotions, and probably learn to be more honest yourself.

Almost everyone you meet tells little white lies. These are the stories that do not usually cause harm. They could be the "fish that got away story" where each time you tell it, the fish gets bigger and bigger. Or it's the lie about how much you really paid for that dress. In most cases, lies are told for several basic reasons.

A lie could be told to impress someone. Maybe you're on a date, and you're looking to win over the affections of your love interest, or perhaps you're on a job interview, and you want to stand out separate from the other candidates.

Other lies are told as a means of deflecting the other person from learning the truth. Perhaps you've had a questionable past, and you want to move in a more positive direction, or you are planning a surprise party for a friend, and you don't want them to find out.

Then there are lies to hide secrets. You may have stolen those supplies from work, or you failed to complete your task, and now it's behind schedule.

The reality is that people tell lies for all sorts of reasons. In most cases, these untruths are harmless and can be overlooked. However, there are times when lies are told about very important matters, the kind that could damage relationships, end careers, or even wind you up behind bars.

It can be considered a self-defense mechanism to be able to detect these types of lies. In fact, lie detection is so important that there are entire careers and a host of technological devices dedicated entirely to uncovering that hidden secret. Detecting lies of this magnitude involves looking at micro-expressions, regular facial expressions, reading body language, and following verbal cues to determine if someone is really lying.

What Deception Looks Like

According to some lie detection experts, there are often "tells" that a liar will make when he is fabricating a story, and they can be seen in three major areas.

1. Signs of nervousness

2. Chemical reactions in the body

3. Physical reactions in the body

One of the first things you must do to tell if a person is lying is to start with a base truth. This is why when given a lie detector test; people are usually first asked to tell something truthfully while they are hooked up to the machine. This is then used as a base for how a person's body normally reacts to truthful situations.

You, however, won't have a lie detector machine to establish a baseline so you will need to use other tactics to establish one. First, and foremost, you will start by engaging the person in regular conversation. During that conversation, you will make small talk and ask basic, non-threatening questions and then observe the person's reactions.

These could be questions like:

- What's your name?

- How old are you?

- Where are you from?

- Are you married?

These are rarely questions people will lie about. The longer you engage that person in conversation, the easier it will be to see how to react to truthful situations. If the person has a normal mannerism, you will immediately notice a nervous tic during a conversation. Now, you have a baseline to gauge their behavior with as you delve deeper into the conversation. Here are a few things you can do to uncover the lie.

Watch the eyes

The eyes tell a lot about how honest a person is. Generally, when a person is lying his eyes will dart from one side to the other. It makes them appear as if they are looking for an escape route. It is a physiological reaction that shows you that he is uncomfortable or he feels trapped by the lie he has told.

They will also avoid making direct eye contact and will look down at the floor or away from you. It will seem as if they feel if they look directly at you, you will uncover their secret.

Lying causes stress and when you're stressed, your eyes will blink more quickly. In a normal situation, a person blinks once every 10 to 12 seconds. However, as the level of stress increases, the frequency of blinking also increases. You may notice that he blinks four to six times in rapid succession.

You should also pay attention to how long they keep their eyes closed. In a normal conversation, a person may close their eyes for only a few milliseconds, but when they are lying, the eyes will be closed for long stretches of time. If you notice that they close their eyes for a second or more, chances are he's spinning you a tall tale.

The direction of the eyes also tells a lot too. In normal situations, right-handed people will look up and to the right if they are telling the truth. They are accessing their memory banks in the brain to retrieve the right information. However, if their gaze is up and to the left, they are tapping into their imagination center of the brain and literally are creating a story.

Researchers say that this happens in the opposite if you are talking to a left-handed person and some people will look neither to the left or the right when they recall a factual event.

If they start to look down and to the right in the direction of their nose, they are creating a lie about smells or other sensory stimulation. The eyes are shifting down and to the left is a sign that he recalls a true memory.

Watch for the fake smile

No matter where you are from, a smile is a frequent sign of welcome and acceptance. More often than not, people will smile even when they don't really feel like they want to but because it is expected. Think of the number of times you smile every day, on job interviews, at social gatherings, at public events, when you meet new people. Since a smile is basically a sign of happiness, it is hard to believe that you are genuinely happy in all those situations. Most of the time, people simply fake it because they are expected to.

Because the smile is such an important gesture when interacting with other people, we need to pay more attention to how it is done. There's no doubt that smiling makes you look better, appear more approachable, and friendlier.

It is a very natural gesture and is very hard to fake. When done properly, you will notice smile lines as the skin bunches up around the eyes. When the smile is fake, these lines won't appear, the smile only appears around the mouth area, but the rest of the face remains lax.

To tell a fake smile, you must also be able to identify a real one. With a real smile, the whole face lights up. This is because you engage many more face muscles. In a real smile, you will see the cheeks enlarge, and the teeth are exposed. This muscle engagement is the voluntary part of a smile. However, other muscles activate involuntarily that are also engaged in a real smile.

The enlarged cheeks are caused by the orbicularis oculus muscle as it contracts and pulls the skin into wrinkles around the outer edge of the eyes (crow's feet). The eyes will close slightly as the chin is pulled upwards.

Now, that you understand what's involved in a real smile, it is easy to identify a fake one. Look for these three things.

1. Eyes are open. There will be no movement in the upper portion of the face with a fake smile.

2. No crow's feet.

3. Bottom teeth are visible. With a genuine smile, the zygomatic muscle is engaged. This is the muscle that controls the mouth. When we smile naturally, this muscle moves upwards, but when we are faking a smile, we often overcorrect and end up moving a muscle outwards exposing the bottom teeth.

It is very important that you understand that there are also variations to this. Some people will have a genuine smile in all sorts of situations whereas others are less inclined to do so when they don't feel it. Being able to identify a genuine smile will help you know if someone is really happy to see you or is just putting on a pretense. By knowing how someone really feels it can help you to know where you stand in any given situation.

Watch the Face

Another nervous habit that many people do when lying is touching their face. It is almost as if the body is fighting against the falsehood and suddenly their face begins to itch. Researchers say this is the result of a chemical reaction that occurs in the body when you lie. To counteract this discomfort, there will be an increased amount of touching of the face and throat, and they may end up doing a lot of scratching on the nose or behind the ear. One place they won't touch is areas around the heart or the chest, especially with an open hand.

Even the lips will reveal their secrets. You might see them pursue their lips as they try to tell their story. This is mainly because of one of the many chemical reactions they may experience when they lie. The mouth will begin to feel dry and cottony. As a result, they will pursue their lips sometimes to the point that they will appear pinched up and white around the edges. This is to counteract the unpleasant reaction. They could also start making a sucking sound as this will force the mouth to create more saliva to overcome the problem.

What Deception Sounds Like

Most of us have heard about an optical illusion. These are the strange scientific phenomena that make us believe something is really happening even though the situation is entirely different. The road where you can literally roll a ball uphill or when you look at a picture, and it appears to be moving. These illusions are simply the result of the brain making assumptions about what the eye is really seeing.

Many do not realize that there are also auditory illusions that can play tricks on your mind as well. Whether you're trying to detect a lie in someone you care about or are trying to determine if a stranger can be trustworthy, there are definitely tell-tale signs of a lie in the voice of the speaker.

Change in pitch or tone: Practiced liars can spin a tale that can sound very convincing to the untrained ear. But if you listen carefully, you'll find the clues in the voice. If you listen closely to the voice of the speaker, you will notice that when they lie, the pitch gets higher than normal or the tone will drop lower than usual. You will also notice that they will speak much faster than normal when they are trying to pull a fast one on you.

If the lie is well rehearsed, you may find that they don't speak in their same manner. Their words will come out measured as if they are speaking to a beat or they may sound like they are reading a script. Even if the story sounds really convincing, these vocal changes will be a strong indication that the story they're telling you is just that—a story.

What Deception Sounds Like: The Unintended Message

At this point, it is important for us to stop and consider our interactions with people. Now that we are beginning to understand how our mannerisms and behavior affect the messages we're trying to send, it is worth it for us to stop and look at what kind of messages we are sending people. Often, people pick up on negative cues without ever really knowing how we understood. This is a universal language that is spoken in all cultures and regions of the earth.

Go back to those days as a child when you just knew you were in trouble whether your parents said anything or not. We learn to pick up on these cues as young children, and we grow into them as we get older. What you are learning in this book, however, is how to take that basic knowledge a step further and rather than picking up on these cues by osmosis, we are now beginning to deliberately look for signals that will reveal even more information about someone.

Numerous factors can have a powerful effect on what we are trying to say to those around us. In face-to-face communication, our behavioral characteristics will have a powerful impact on how people respond to us. Our facial expressions, the tone of voice, and mannerisms are sending a message whether we want to or not.

As you go about your day, stop and ask yourself what message you are really sending. If you're speaking positive words but your actions show that you are feeling anxious or stressed, it is worth it to stop to analyze your situation. If you've been wondering why people are standoffish with you or have some other type of negative response to your kindness, it just might be that you're sending an unintended message that goes contrary to your goals.

From now on, whenever you interact with others, it should be with a sense of purpose. Make sure that you are not selling the lie that you're trying to uncover. This will be very beneficial in all sorts of situations. Try to take an outside view of whatever is happening, and chances are you'll be able to uncover the hidden message that is found in every aspect of your own environment.

Hearing More Than Words

One step below outright lying is the misunderstanding. We've heard these complaints many times, especially from those who are closest to us. "She said it was okay that I didn't get home on time but now she's really angry and won't speak to me." Obviously, the other party thought he understood what she meant but was very wrong.

This type of situation could have easily been avoided if he had learned to read more than the words she was relating to him in the conversation. You have to listen to the whole body when you are communicating with someone. This means looking at the micro-expressions, listening to the tone and pitch of the voice, the choice of words they make, and even the order of the words presented.

It seems like a pretty straightforward way to get to the truth of something, but it is not always the easiest thing that can be done.

Still, don't get too wrapped up in the message and assume that you're on a mission to decode the language someone is giving to you. True— there are many hidden meanings in every conversation. Rather than thinking of it as a code, think of it as a puzzle. The words people speak are just one aspect of the feature. With those words, you get a single snapshot of a single minute of a day. But when you add a few more pieces to the puzzle, the picture becomes even clearer. Take these two spoken sentences as an example. You'll notice that where you decide to pause can change the entire meaning of the words. The words used are the same with no deviation, but the message is very different.

We're going to eat, John.

In this sentence, there is a pause after the word "eat." This is letting John know that it's time to eat and that's what is intended.

We're going to eat John.

In this sentence, John needs to be very concerned. Without the pause, the message is that the intention is actually to eat John. Rather than having him over for dinner, it sounds like John is on the menu. While this example is extreme, the concept is very clear. There are many hidden innuendos in between words that need to be factored into your analysis. Without utilizing the pause, you may be sending out an unintended hidden message that you don't want anyone to know.

Chapter 4: Reading the Lie

Here is another example.

Mary loves me. In this example, the young man is happy that Mary is in love with him.

Does Mary love me? Here, with the emphasis on "loves," his tone is much sharper, perhaps a little higher than usual. He is asking a question indicating that he is in doubt. If he says this with a surprised facial expression of wide eyes, raised eyebrows, you would be positive that he's not talking about the fact that Mary loves him but about the surprise to learn that she loves him.

Mary love **ME!** In this expression, the stress is put on the word "me." Followed by an exclamation point, you can imagine a raised voice. This message could mean that he is defensive, possibly even angry. The message is clear, Mary loves him, not you.

Now, taking this a step further. If you're an outsider witnessing this conversation, what conclusions will you draw? Do you have the entire story or are you missing some of the hidden clues?

Understanding the spoken message is simply a matter of matching the right emotion to the right situations. It is not a code in the sense that every word has a single meaning. With that concept, we wouldn't be much better than animals. In reality, we have many definitions and messages for the same words. Scientists have come to understand that language is not just something we learn as we grow older but is actually encoded in our DNA. We naturally decode the messages we can pick up but to be able to read and analyze people truly, we need to start looking for those hidden messages that we aren't noticing. This is a major way of learning to read people and become better communicators in the process.

Learning Communication Styles

Learning the different ways to communicate can also help you be able to read people. We all need to recognize these different styles that we use in our daily interactions. There are five different ways that people communicate with one another. We'll look at each one and show you in which areas of life you are most likely to see these communication styles put into place. As you will see every method of communication is not appropriate for every type of situation, so it makes sense that everyone will be able to master several different communication styles so that their interactions will fit the scenario.

We often label a person as assertive or passive-aggressive without giving it much thought. Unlike individual characteristics, communication styles can be adopted by all different personalities. They are the way we are trained to handle different situations, so they are interchangeable. Let's take a closer look at each of them.

1. Assertive

Those who show an assertive communication style tend to have a high level of self-esteem. It is considered to be one of the healthiest ways to communicate. It strikes a perfect balance between being too easy going and too aggressive. People who are assertive are confident and are less likely to try to manipulate a situation with lies. They know their limits and won't permit others to push them beyond a point they are capable of. These people won't try to make you feel guilty because someone else has a need or a want, nor will they be so hard-hearted that they aren't able to show empathy to those when the situation calls for it.

Behaviors of an Assertive person

- Can reach their goals without taking advantage of other people.

- Knows how to protect their own rights and respect others at the same time.

- Comfortable in social situations and are emotionally balanced.

- Can make their own decisions and will accept responsibility for the consequences.

- Will ask for what they want or need but are willing to accept rejection.

- Doesn't deflect compliments but can accept them graciously.

Non-Verbal Characteristics

- Their voice holds a medium pitch, moderate speed, and volume.

- They have an open posture, are balanced, stand tall, and can relax without fidgeting.

- They have even but expressive gestures that are well rounded.

- They make good eye contact when speaking with you.

- They respect other people's boundaries.

Language

- They are polite when making a request.

- They will explain what they need rather than just ask for it.

- They are apologetic when necessary.

When you are interacting with an assertive person, you will naturally feel that you can trust them. They will make you feel like you know exactly where you stand and you will feel as if you can easily accept their criticisms as well as their compliments. They are self-reliant and respectful of others around them.

2. Aggressive

The aggressive person is focused on winning and nothing else. They don't really give much thought to what their actions will cause another person as their primary focus is to get their needs met. They often believe that their rights are more important and that their contributions are more valuable than anyone else's. Their way of interacting with people is often by intimidation and fear, and the actual message they deliver is often not received because people are usually focused on the way it is delivered rather than the point itself.

Behaviors of an Aggressive person

- Often loud and hostile.

- Threatening, ready to fight (verbally or physically).

- In it to win no matter the cost.

- Abrasive and demanding.

- Stubborn and willful.

- Unpredictable and at times displays an explosive temperament.

- Intimidating.

- Bully.

Non-Verbal Characteristics

- Loud voice, shouting.

- Posture is usually overbearing, making them bigger than others.

- Large expansive gesturing.

- Sharp and jerking movements.

- Their faces usually wear a scowl, frown, or they are glaring.

- They frequently invade the personal space of others.

- They crowd others and try to stand over them, looking down on others.

Language

- Insulting.

- Demanding.

- At times offensive.

- Demeaning.

- Often sarcastic, threatening, blaming, calling people derogatory names.

When you are interacting with an aggressive person, you are likely to become defensive or react aggressively in return. You'll feel the pull to be resistant and uncooperative, resentful, and a host of negative feelings will come out. At times they may make you feel humiliated or fearful, and many lose their respect for them. People often tried to hide the truth from aggressive people because they are fearful of the reaction they might receive. Others may avoid them because they feel they are being "railroaded" into complying with situations they are not comfortable with.

3. **Passive-Aggressive**

The passive-aggressive person is deceitful. They may appear to be submissive or complaint on the surface, but in reality, they are showing their anger and frustration more indirectly. People who are passive-aggressive usually feel powerless in their circumstances. As a result, they have built up a great deal of resentment, and the only way they know how to express their feelings is by undermining those they resent by lying. Often the consequences of this behavior end up having a backlash, which can cause them more harm than those they are trying to punish.

Behaviors

- Aggressive behavior is often indirect.

- They are sarcastic and devious.

- They are unreliable.

- Complains a lot.

- Sulky.

- Can be overly patronizing.

- Gossipy.

- Pleasant when speaking to people but trash talks them to others.

- They may do things to cause trouble for another person but never directly confrontational.

Non-Verbal Behavior

- Voice is often overly sweet.

- Asymmetrical posture (stands with their hands on their hips or they stand with their hips thrust out while talking).

- Quick and quirky gestures.

- Often looks very sweet and innocent.

- Stands too close to others, even touching them as they pretend to be friendly.

Language

- Often speaks as if they are okay with the idea or suggestion.

- Demeans their own ideas in front of others.

- Sarcastic.

- Self-deprecating.

When you interact with a passive-aggressive, you are likely to feel confused by their mixed signals, angry at the way the switch from one side to the other, maybe even feel hurt and resentful as you learn you cannot trust them.

4. Submissive

Those who are submissive are focused entirely on pleasing other people to avoid conflict. They often put other people's needs above their own and will forgo their rights for the sake of others. They do not feel that their own needs and rights are as important and feel that they have little or nothing worthwhile to contribute to any situation.

Behavior

- They are frequently apologizing for even the smallest of infractions.

- They act as if they are imposing when they have to ask for something they need or want.

- They will go to great lengths to avoid confrontation.

- They find it hard to accept responsibility or make decisions.

- They give in to other's preferences while neglecting their own.

- They tend to choose not to do something rather than get involved.

- They have a victim mentality.

- Not comfortable with accepting compliments.

- Afraid to express their feelings or desires.

- Non-Verbal Behavior

- They speak with a soft voice.

- They try to make themselves appear as small as possible physically.

- They fidget a lot and make small gestures.

- Avoids eye contact.

- Reluctant to take the initiative.

Language

- They use dismissive words that don't reflect positively on themselves.

- They often will give up easily rather than confront a situation head-on.

- They will often defer to another person rather than to give their own opinion.

Dealing with a submissive person can make you feel exasperated and frustrated. These people tend to make you feel guilty if you buy into their victim mentality. They cause you to let your guard down, and when that happens, they can take advantage of your good nature. There is usually low energy surrounding them which makes others feel resentful. Many will give up trying to help them because they often have a defeatist attitude, so there are no positive results.

5. Manipulative

Those who are manipulative tend to scheme and plot a lot. They are calculating and shrewd. These are people who are skilled at getting people to yield to their will. All of this is done without outwardly expressing their needs and desires. They speak to you openly, but there is usually a hidden message in the meaning of what they say.

Behavior

- These people are cunning and controlling in a seemingly unobtrusive way.

- They may sulk around you.

- They do not directly ask for things but will ask in a roundabout way.

- They can make others feel obliged to help them.

- May resort to "crocodile tears" or fake crying to gain your sympathy.

Non-Verbal Behavior

- They may use a high-pitched voice that is patronizing and ingratiating.

- They walk around with a sad expression

Language

- They will use an expression that compliments you for something they want.

- They will be apologetic or make excuses for why they didn't get something that others may have.

- They will be self-deprecating to gain sympathy.

It is very important to understand and be able to identify these different communication styles. Being able to recognize these people when you see them will help you to be able to respond effectively to any given situation. This knowledge can also help you to recognize if you have any of these tendencies in yourself.

While there are some people, who tend to lean more towards one communication style over the others, most of us have a blend of these characteristics that we can pull out at any time depending on the circumstances. Keep in mind that everyone has a choice as to which style they choose to use in any given situations. Being assertive is often the preferred style of communication, but other situations may call for different factors.

If you are at work, it may be necessary for you to show some assertiveness but if you're in a hostage situation, being submissive may be the best response needed. We've seen people become master manipulators in many situations: a woman breaking out in tears after she is told no for something she wants, or an employer being overly demanding when he wants a certain deadline to be met. There is room for all of the communication styles everywhere you go, so if you're really serious about being able to read people, it is more important than ever that you learn how to assess situations before deciding which type of personality is best suited for the circumstances.

Chapter 5:
Body Language

Up until this point, our focus has been on verbal and non-verbal cues and hidden messages in our mannerisms. We've learned that gestures are a key element in communication. However, few people realize that these gestures, facial tics, and other idiosyncrasies are just a smaller picture of body language.

When you understand body language, you will be able to uncover many different hidden messages in communicating with people. For example, you will be able to identify when someone is lying, feels uncomfortable, or they have an aggressive personality.

How to Analyze People

Researchers believe that as much as 80% of our communication needs are done through body language, and words make up only 20%. The way we use our bodies to communicate can be truly fascinating. It may seem impossible at first, but it is essential to understanding people, what motivates and encourages them so you can learn exactly how they truly feel.

In truth, every part of the body is involved in communication. Once you begin to grasp the hidden signals that people are sending, it will be like uncovering clues that can enhance your life. As a result, you will have better relationships in every aspect of your life. You will be able to tell when someone is uncomfortable or when they are overconfident. You will know when they are interested in what you have to say or when you have lost your audience.

Chapter 5: Body Language

To accurately be able to read someone's body language though, you will need to establish a baseline again. As you go through this chapter, you will find that the signals we'll discuss here can change based on the context of the situation. In other words, they are not always absolute. For example, some people may be in the habit of folding their arms in front of their body. Most books you read will tell you that this is a sign of stubbornness, which the person is blocking themselves off from you, and is not receptive. However, in some environments, it could mean something entirely different. They may be cold, and it is a subconscious need to get warm, they could be uncomfortable in their situation, or they may have just heard some bad news and are applying a self-comforting gesture.

The same could be said of someone who stands with their hands on their hips. To the onlooker, it may appear to be a dominating attitude, and that they are attempting to be overbearing. However, it may simply be an indication of someone in deep thought, analyzing a situation for themselves. The reality is that body language could mean a myriad of things so taking them in context could be just as revealing as the information itself. We have seen this to be true in other areas of communication, so it just makes sense that it is true in body language as well.

Gestures - What Do They Really Mean?

Let's start by looking at each area of the body to see what message they could be sending when you are trying to communicate with someone.

The Head: We may not realize it, but one of the first things our eyes gravitate to is the head. We automatically look at the hair and make a judgment. Think about it. If you see a person whose hair is unkempt—perhaps not combed or disheveled in some way—what is your first reaction? Depending on the time of day it is, you may think that he has just woken up, or is trying to separate himself from the world.

When people go into a state of depression, one of the first things they start to neglect is their grooming. While bed-head may be an acceptable appearance for a loving partner, someone who spends the entire day without taking care of his hair is someone with some negative energy flowing around him.

On the other hand, when the person is well-groomed, and their hair is clean, it gives you a feeling that you can trust that person. They are professional, and they take their role seriously. The brain does all of these analyses in a tiny fraction of a second. Now, let's look at some other forms of body language when you are trying to communicate with someone. Remember, at first glance; you've already formed an opinion about the kind of person they are. Now you want to see if your opinion will remain as you try to communicate with them.

The head-shake: When someone rotates their head from side to side, it doesn't always mean "no." The same is true for the head nod. It doesn't always mean that the person agrees with you. Here are a few things you might want to factor into your analysis. The speed and the rhythm of the motion will tell you what the person is thinking. A fast rhythm shake usually does indicate a lack of agreement. A slow shaking or if they turn their head unusually or irregularly generally means they are struggling to understand your meaning. In this case, you may need to clarify your point. A slow, rhythmic shake usually means they don't believe you. They are struggling to accept the reality of what you have just said.

When the head shake is only slightly visible, you barely discern movement, or you only see a half shake of the head, it could indicate disbelief and surprise. It might appear that your words just slapped the person in the face and they were unprepared for what they heard. Another gesture or movement of the head that you should learn is something called the "cut-off." This occurs when you are engaged in a conversation and the person you are talking to turns their head away from you. This can be a signal that they are annoyed by what you are saying or that they find the content of your information disturbing.

It is important to understand though, that every turn of the head does not mean they are not interested. At times, people may turn their head away to contemplate and give serious thought to what you are saying. So, let's see how we can tell the difference.

When people are thinking about something serious and important, it is natural for them to stare far off into the distance. This far away gaze helps to improve the depth of their concentration and think more clearly. They are actually blocking out all stimulation from their immediate surroundings and concentrating on the matter. If they turn away and have that far-away stare, it could be that they are taking your message seriously.

However, if they don't like what they are hearing, they will try to disengage contact and take steps to break off the conversation. You will see the cut off is often accompanied by other gestures that show impatience and frustration. They may start glancing off to other parts of the room, begin to fiddle with other objects nearby, or they may start to throw in meaningless or sarcastic remarks in an attempt to change the conversation.

There is also the head bobble, which doesn't seem to be saying yes or no. This movement can be quite confusing. Depending on where you are from, it can appear differently than what you are accustomed to. So, if you're often interacting with people from other regions of the earth, it helps to know the different head bobbles. In the Balkan countries, you'll find that even the nodding for yes and the shaking for no is different. Their head gestures are actually the opposite of the rest of the world. The head bobble is when the person moves his head vertically and from side to side at the same time. It appears to be a combination of both the nod and the shake being done simultaneously.

The wobble is usually done without any verbal cues as to its meaning and is most commonly seen in people from Southeast Asia, so when a westerner is faced with this odd gesture, they are not entirely sure what to think. But it does have a purpose in a conversation, and once you learn it, you might find yourself trying to do it too. In its most general of uses, it can mean "I got it" or "I understand." Or it can simply mean that they feel your comments are "good." It can also mean "yes" in answer to a question you've just asked. It can be a form of thank you, a word that is not commonly used in that part of the world. It can be used to acknowledge someone's presence, almost the same as a nod in greeting in western cultures. It is a form of greeting to a stranger in a public place (train, plane, bus, restaurant, etc.).

There are different head bobbles that you may come across:

- When it is fast and continuous, it is a sign that the person really understands your message. The more energy applied to the wobbling, the better they understand you.

- When the head moves quickly from one side to the other, it means "alright" or "okay."

- When it is slow and soft, it is a sign of respect or that they see you as a friend.

Here are a few other head gestures you are likely to see:

- When the head moves back and forth rather than side to side, it is generally a sign of disagreement.

- When the head is tilted up, it means they are genuinely interested in what you have to say.

- When the head is tilted down it means they have developed a negative attitude towards you that could also be a sign of aggression. Try to imagine the position a bull takes before it attacks.

The Torso: A person's posture when they are interacting with you can also say a lot about them, especially in the torso. When the back is straight, and they are standing tall, their neck is high and upright, and their shoulders are straight and not pushing forward or hunching down it is a strong sign of self-confidence. It gives the impression of someone being in complete control. If you notice that the person has drooping shoulders and torso sags around the middle, it could be a sign that the person is trying to play upon your sympathies and is silently asking you for help.

This sympathy plea is fine on occasion, but if you find you're interacting with someone who has this posture all the time, it is not a good thing. It could mean that they are simply manipulating you, and they are playing on your good nature, but it could also mean they have some underlying health condition that should be addressed.

You might not think that the torso—since it doesn't move much—can say a lot but you'd be wrong. By observing how a person positions their torso, you can tell if they respect you and are interested in what you have to say. The next time you're engaged in conversation with someone, look for these communication signs.

- When the torso is facing you, it generally means that they are interested and they want to connect with you on some level.

- When the torso is slightly tilted away from you (perhaps at a 45-degree angle), it's a sign that they are beginning to lose interest. They are looking for a way to get out of the conversation.

- If they are completely turned away, either to the side or turning their backs in your direction, consider yourself dismissed.

- If the torso is leaning in your direction, it shows that they are keenly interested in your message. They naturally want to pull in closer as if they are trying to get more of what you are saying.

- When they are leaning away from you, it means they have an aversion to you or your topic of discussion. However, if they are in a seated position and leaning backward, but their legs are stretched in your direction, they are still engaged in the conversation. This movement is simply a means of them getting comfortable.

- If they have crossed their arms over their chest, it usually means that they disagree with your point of view. Keep in mind that this gesture is usually disguised so you'll have to look for it. It could be seen as a man playing with his cufflinks or someone holding a drink across the torso. If possible, some people will hide their torso behind another object to create the same signal. For example, standing behind a chair or a table or bar of some kind. The general idea is that they are blocking the torso from you.

• When the torso is wide open, laying backward in a comfortable position, the chest is inflated and open; it generally means that the person feels superior to you. He has taken a position of dominance over you. Be careful.

Arms and Hands: The movement of the arms and hands also carry a great deal of significance in an interaction. The hands can especially say a lot about the person's emotional state of mind. For example, a person who is nervously fidgeting or fumbling with objects could be very bored or anxious about something. Arms positioned on the hips with the elbows pointing outward can reveal an air of arrogance, even if that is not their intention. In fact, many hidden messages can be picked up when watching arm and hand gestures.

- Crossed arms generally are an attempt to hold in the feelings or to block other people from getting too close. It is like putting up a roadblock to prevent the conversation from entering a place that makes them feel uncomfortable.

- When the arms are folded across the heart, it is often an attempt to protect themselves from getting hurt (mostly emotionally). This is a gesture that even monkeys and chimps do when faced with a frontal attack.

Studies have shown that when a person crosses his arms, he also closes his mind. So, he is not listening any longer to the information presented. Research has shown that the retention of those who listen to lectures with crossed arms is around 40% less than those who listen with a more open and welcoming posture.

- Men and women cross their arms differently. Men tend to rotate the arms slightly inward while women tend to rotate them outward. You'll notice that women tend to keep their arms more open when around men they are attracted to and will cross their arms in front of their breasts when they are not attracted.

- When both arms are folded across the chest, it is an attempt to put up a barrier against something they don't like. This can also mean they disagree with what they are hearing. Even if the person verbally agrees with your comments, he is not buying your story. To counteract this, try to find out what it is they disagree with or give them something to hold: a pen, a drink, or something that will require them to unfold their arms. Remember, when the arms are crossed so is the mind. If you can get them to unfold their arms, you have a much better chance of them listening to your point of view and winning them back over to your side.

- When the fists are clenched at the end of the folded arms, it indicates anger and hostility. Combine this with a tight-lipped smile and a red face, and you can be pretty sure you're being threatened.

- When the person grips their arms with both hands, it is usually an attempt to avoid exposure to the body. You might see them gripping their arms very tightly, so much so that the fingers and the knuckles of the hands start to turn white. This is a self-comforting mechanism. It shows an attitude that is both negative and restrained.

- Arm folding can also be a sign of a lower position or status. Those who consider themselves superior to you may choose to keep their hands behind their backs in an open stance while those who are subordinate will cross their arms in the presence of a superior. Those who feel they have an equal status might cross their arms with the thumbs pointing upward even if the other party does not agree.

This gesture is a sign that he feels in control and has a lot of self-confidence but still at the same time shielding himself from someone else.

This gesture, when given along with other positive gestures, is a signal that the person is ready to ask for a commitment. A good cue for salesmen to zero in and try to "close the deal." However, if you get the arms cross with clenched fists, it could mean that you need to resolve some issues before you attempt.

The Half-Hug: You learned the half-hug when you were a child when your parents comforted you when something traumatic happened. Perhaps you skinned your knee, or you took a tumble that caused you distress. Your parents didn't give you a full hug but wrapped a single arm around you to console you. We adopt this gesture as adults by self-comforting ourselves by pulling one arm across the belly and grasping the other arm tightly with the hand. This single arm barrier can be seen in both professional and domestic situations where there is a sense of insecurity or anxiety. It is more often seen in women than it is in men, but it is a universal sign that you see in all cultures.

The Fig Leaf: The male equivalent of the half hug is men holding hands with themselves and holding them over their genital area as if to protect the "crown jewels" from harm. You will notice this position in many areas when they have to wait in line to receive government benefits of some kind. You'll see it in homeless shelters and other areas where they are more likely to find themselves feeling vulnerable.

It really doesn't matter how you see it. Any time there is a crossing of the arms it is considered to be a negative gesture and the message it sends is one of insecurity. They may disguise it in some form or fashion, but any time one arm crosses the body towards the other arm, it can be seen as building a barrier between you and the other person. If you want to be openly received and accepted in any situation, make sure that you choose ahead of time not to cross your arms when dealing with people.

Hand Gestures: Hand gestures are a natural part of communication. Encoded in our DNA, even small children learn how to use hand gestures before they can talk well. They help to build communication especially in cases where words cannot fully express a thought. Research shows that hand gestures can actually increase the understanding of a message by as much as 60%. We are actually born to speak with our hands. It is a sign of intelligence, and it is a very effective way of getting people to listen to you. It can almost put people into a hypnotic state as they focus on the gestures. They begin to tune in more deeply to the words you say. If you don't believe this, then think of how mesmerized people become when they watch a sign language interpreter at work. While they don't know the meaning of the signs, it is as if they can't take their eyes off of it.

When learning to use hand gestures, it is important that you follow certain basic rules to be more effectively understood.

- Hand gestures are usually performed inside of an invisible box. The box usually goes from the waist to the top of your chest, and from side to side. Anytime you gesture outside of this box it can become a distraction rather than a way to enhance the conversation.

- Try to stay in the middle of the spectrum. Hand gestures that are low energy and stiff usually will reflect a negative vibe while those that have high energy and overly expressive can be overwhelming to the viewer.

- Your gestures should be purposeful. Each gesture should have a purpose of enhancing the message you're trying to deliver.

- Know exactly what you're saying with your hands. If you're planning a presentation, just as you prepare your words carefully. Plan your gestures too.

- Make them smooth and avoid choppy movements. When there is no fluidity in your gestures, it can be distracting. When the movements are smooth and relaxed people will be drawn to you.

- Limit your use of hand gestures when communicating with people from other countries. Not all of them are universal. For example, the offensive middle finger often used as an insult in the western world actually means "brother" in many eastern countries. Make sure you choose neutral and universal gestures when dealing with other cultures. At least, until you know if your gestures won't be viewed as offensive.

Before you go full scale on hand gestures, it is a good idea to watch other people and observe how others in that culture use their gestures. As you develop the skill for that region, you'll find that you will be able to communicate a lot better without ever fully knowing the native language. Remember, of all the body language movements you should understand, hand gestures should be at the top of your list.

- Listing: This gesture lets the viewer know that the details of a particular list are very important. People do this in different ways, they may count out loud as they point to each finger on their list, or they may just raise one finger as they say a number of an item on their list. This is a visual aid that makes it easier for the viewer to recall the points.

- A little: If you want to emphasize a small amount or indicate the small size of something, you show it. Usually by placing the tip of the index finger and the thumb together.

- Listen: You see teachers do this in the classroom when they want the students to settle down. It is the clapping of the hands together that creates a sound that will automatically draw attention. Some people clap the palms of the hands together while others will slap the back of one hand into the palm of another. The key is to blend the sound and the motion together.

- Determination: Making a solid fist and shaking it or punching it in the air is a sign of intensity.

- Everything: The movement of sweeping across a surface in front of you with open hands and palms facing outward is a sign that you are referring to it all. This gesture can also mean to clear something away, depending on the context of the conversation.

- Size: Size can be indicated by showing the level of something. Imagine patting the top of a child's head. Small would be lower, a medium size would be about waist high, and tall would be, perhaps, shoulder-high.

- Wisdom: By gently tapping the fingertips together, you give a signal that you are well grounded. It is a sign of wisdom and can be very calming to both the user and the viewer.

- The finger-shake: Pointing is not always accepted with grace so use this gesture with caution. This gesture is often considered to be accusatory or offensive even if it is not intended to be. But when you point your finger and shake it, it can be viewed as a scolding or reprimand. This gesture needs to be read in the context of the situation as it can have many different meanings.

- We/Us: This gesture is often used when you are in a group of people, and it indicates that what you're saying is all-inclusive. Simply open your arms wide as if you're about to hug them and give them an invisible embrace. If you're in a one-on-one situation, you can gently place the palm of your hand on their back to let them know that you are included in their inner circle.

- Stop A universal gesture made by pushing the palm towards the person you want to stop. You can do this while someone is speaking and you'll notice that the reaction is almost immediate. They will stop and direct their attention towards you. It is important that you use this gesture sparingly as it can be offensive if used too frequently or in the wrong situations.

By understanding how to use hand gestures effectively, you will be able to easily see just what someone else is saying when you're interacting with them. Hand gestures are probably the most common form of physical communication used worldwide. Many (not all) are common and consistent throughout the world. Even those who are blind from birth have used hand gestures to enhance their communication, which makes it easy to understand why it is such an integral part of communication throughout the world.

Legs

Another area of the body to watch carefully are the legs. The majority of people tend to be less aware of the messages our legs send when interacting with other people. However, if we pay just the slightest bit of attention, we'll learn a great deal about a person's intrinsic feelings about a given situation. One of the advantages of observing leg movements is because few people are aware of the hidden messages they tell, it is rare that someone would try to fake a leg position to send a message as they might try with a smile.

Observing leg movements involves more than just watching how a person stands. You can learn a lot about by how they walk and any micro-muscular movements they may do in their lower extremities. It is a natural tendency to move towards the things we want or like and to move away from those that cause us discomfort or anxiety. Keeping these basic rules in mind can help you to decode the hidden messages people send with their legs.

1. The Parallel Stance

When you stand with the legs straight, and the feet close together, it is a position of subordination. It is one of the most vulnerable positions to stand in. Because the body is not perfectly balanced, another person can easily push them over without much effort. This stance is often used by people who are insecure about their position within a certain group. The wider the stance, the more solid the foundation they stand on.

2. The Legs Open and Apart

The wider stance is predominantly a male position. It gives them a firm foundation to stand on and makes for a strong posture that is difficult to move. You see army soldiers do this all the time when they are standing guard. It is a sign of dominance or authority of another person. If ever, you are feeling less than yourself, try taking this position and see how your mood changes. Stand with your feet spread apart, shoulders back, and your head held high, and soon you'll pick up a more positive mood.

3. The Pose

Have you ever noticed when people pose for pictures one of the first things they'll do is stick one leg out and towards the camera? The poser puts the bulk of his weight on one leg and "presents" the other leg with the inner thigh exposed. The feet are turned outward so that more of the inner leg is exposed. This is the softer, and most erogenous area of the leg. This pose reveals a lot of things. Because we point our front foot in the direction, our mind is focused on it tells the viewer that this is something they are very interested in. In a group, the foot will automatically point to the person they find to be most interesting. If it is pointed towards the exit, it indicates that they are ready to leave.

4. The Scissor Stance

Standing with your legs crossed is often seen when in a group of people you may not know very well. When the legs are open it shows confidence and dominance but crossing the legs means you're closed off, defensive, or are in unfamiliar territory. It is also a means of protecting the genital area. Women use it to send the message that access is denied while men may use it to protect their masculinity.

It is easy to mistake the scissor stance for someone who may be cold. It is natural for people to cross their legs and arms when they are cold. However, you can easily tell the difference. When someone is cold, they will cross their arms and tuck their hands higher up. Rather than crossing them down by the waist they will cross their arms closer to the armpits to warm them. The legs will be crossed but will remain relatively straight, stiff, and pressed tightly against the other leg.

5. The Leg Cross

In a seated position, one leg crossed over the other can be a sign that they are emotionally withdrawn from the conversation. They are not interested in what is being said and are attempting to block themselves off from any continued discussion.

There is also the figure four cross leg position, done primarily by men. This is where the leg is crossed so that they resemble the number four where the ankle of the crossed leg rests on top of the bottom leg. Men who use this posture are viewed as more relaxed and in control. While not seen very often, women use this posture only around other women, and it sends the same signal.

A downside to this position is that it is not widely accepted in the Middle East or Asia because it shows the sole of the shoe, which is considered to be highly offensive.

6. The Leg Clamp

An extension of the figure four leg cross is the leg clamp. The leg is literally locked in a permanent position using the ankles to basically "clamp" it in place. This is a sign that the person is stubborn and competitive and is likely to object to the viewpoint of anyone who does not share their feelings.

There is also a woman's version of the leg clamp where they will lock their ankles but keep the knees held tightly together and the hands resting on top of the upper leg.

Chapter 5: Body Language

By carefully observing what on the surface appears to be natural gestures and body movements, we'll understand what is really going on in the mind of everyone we interact with. It may not be mind-reading per se, but there's no question that all of this knowledge could be used to our benefit when applied correctly.

We have to learn to reach actions rather than words. This will help us to keep our minds opened and focused on what's really in front of us. Body language is so much a part of our lives that it is hard to believe that we have neglected it for so long and struggled. As a result, to really communicate with the people in our lives.

Chapter 6:
Personality Types

O ne final area of analyzing people we will discuss is the different personality types. While each person's personality is very different from someone else's, we can definitely classify them into different types. There are 16 different personality types to identify so it should be relatively easy to be able to slot pretty much anyone you meet into one of them. So, with so many to consider, let's get started.

The Duty Fulfiller

This personality type is almost entirely focused on themselves. They are extreme introverts, so any information they absorb from their environment is judged in a very literal and inflexible fashion. They are extremely logical and tend to be very reserved when around other people. They are, for the most part, loners and prefer to live in a quiet and serene environment whenever possible.

These people live very serious lives and methodically approach everything. They tend to be dependable, loyal, and stress the importance of honesty and integrity in every situation. Because they are so mechanical in their approach to life, they can easily slip into a panic mode when things go wrong and will view all situations very negatively.

The Mechanic

This person is also an introvert and deals with things in a highly logical manner. However, they are keenly interested in not just getting the job done but in how it is done. They prefer to analyze situations and reason on every aspect of it. They are not impressed by theories and opinions if there is no practical application associated with it. They love the mechanical side of things and have a strong affinity for adventure. They work well in high-stress situations and have honed their hand-eye coordination to perfection.

The Nurturer

The nurturer literally accepts stimuli from their environment. They prefer to deal with things that focus on feelings or how they might apply to their value system. They tend to be kind and are focused on solidarity or unity among people. They prefer to be around people who cooperate and work together for the benefit of all. They are extremely sensitive to other people's feelings and can bring out the best in those they interact with.

The nurturer requires a lot of positive reinforcement, and when they don't get it, they can easily slip into a depressive state.

The Artist

The artist's goal is to deal with things through their personal feelings and analyze them based on how they fit into their own system of values. They can be quite creative and are continuously in search of hidden meanings in the things they do. On the outside, everything appears to be in order and efficient; however, internally, they prefer to work intuitively rather than by any specific system or arrangement.

Idealist

This is a very reflective personality. They tend to be quiet and very committed to serving the people around them. They are hard workers who live in harmony with a very personal value system. Those who fit into this category are usually writers and quick thinkers. They can visualize even the remotest of possibilities and find ways to do what others might find impossible.

The Scientist

The scientist is a very original thinker. They are very determined and analytical. Their talents lie in transforming general ideas and theories into real life possibilities. These people love structure, embrace knowledge, and are extremely motivated. They are constantly looking for long-term solutions to problems and not the quick fix. They have very high standards for themselves and for those who they interact with. They have the potential to be natural leaders but are just as content taking the back seat and letting others lead them as well.

Many may find it difficult to interact with a scientist. They tend to be very blunt and abrupt when speaking to others and are often misunderstood.

The Thinker

This personality is very creative but is also logical, a mix rarely found in most people. They can become extremely excited when they hear new ideas and are eager to take on the challenge of building the idea into something workable.

They struggle at times to make friends because they tend to be reserved and quiet and prefer to be alone. They like to work autonomously and would rather not lead, however, they are not inclined to follow someone either. Their world exists almost entirely in their own minds so they are not attached to traditions and rarely are willing to comply with many acceptable standards in the people around them.

The Judge

This personality tends to internalize the events happening around them. They want to understand things based on their own personal feelings about a situation and how it works in their personal life. They are intuitive and are often kind and caring. They are continuously analyzing and reshaping the priorities in their lives to improve on themselves in many ways.

The above personalities are common among introverts. There are another eight that apply primarily to extroverts.

The Doer

This is a high energy, action-oriented person who can be very friendly. They are highly motivated when they receive immediate results and love to take risks. They are not inclined to sit around and listen to long explanations and may break the rules from time to time. They have very good people skills and will shoot from the hip when they need to. They do not hesitate to get their hands dirty if it means they can get the job done faster. As eager as they are, follow-through is often lacking, and they tend to pass the task on to someone else once the excitement of the work has dissipated.

The Guardian

The guardians are very organized but are also conservative. They tend to be drawn more to athletics and will pull away from theoretical conversations if possible. They know exactly what they want and how things should be done, are hardworking and loyal to the people in their lives. They are happy to take on the leadership roles and are excellent organizers.

They prefer peace and would rather live in a world that is logical and practical. Their eyes are continuously scanning their environment to make sure everything is working as it should be. They will do whatever is necessary to make sure work is done the way they think it is supposed to be.

The Performer

Performers are fun-loving and people-oriented. They can find enjoyment just about everywhere they go, and their joy is infectious. They love new experiences and can easily slip into living in the moment. However, they do not like analyzing things or listening to theories.

Performers interact with others and love being the center of attention at social gatherings. They can be very practical and have a powerful common-sense attitude when addressing problems. Performers not only connect easily with people they also have a strong affinity for animals and children and enjoy spending their time in nature.

The Caregiver

These people are warm and tend to be very popular. They have a strong sense of responsibility to care for others. They do, however, need a lot of positive reinforcement to feel good about themselves and the work they do. They gather information about others and then use it to support the people they care for. Their sense of obligation helps them bring out the best in people and to see the world through other people's eyes.

The Inspirer

These are creative people who maintain high energy and enthusiastic view of life. They often excel at work and can handle any task that appeals to their interests. They have powerful people skills and a strong inner value system.

They often appear laid back and relaxed, giving the impression that they do not have a sense of purpose. They relish in new ideas and concepts and detest the hum drum nitty-gritty details behind theories and ideas. Because of their flexibility, they have a wide range of skills and can adjust to a wide range of interests. They live their life on their terms and resent having to do things they do not believe is right.

The Giver

The giver has awesome people skills and is very popular. They take other people's views seriously, and they resent being alone. These are people who view life from the human perspective and prefer to do things that serve others and often place the needs of the people around them above their own. They thrive on intimate relationships, and they need them to maintain their upbeat lifestyle.

The Visionary

The visionary is a natural born leader. They are outspoken and assertive and can understand organizational problems. They use their unique talents to meet challenges that often come up when people work together in groups.

They are great public speakers, and they value those who are knowledgeable and capable, but they have little tolerance for those who tend to be disorganized. Their view of the world is a series of obstacles that must be overcome on a daily basis. They fit very well in the corporate environment.

Whether you're an introvert or an extrovert, there is a perfect slot somewhere that matches your personality. As you read through these descriptions, keep in mind that they are based on the person's innate feelings and viewpoints on life. You might find some people fit with some of the points of each personality listed but if those characteristics are not innate or a part of that person's whole being, then chances are that is not the personality that fits them best.

Conclusion

Thanks for making it through to the end of How to Analyze People: A Beginner's Guide to Analyzing, Understanding, and Predicting People's Behavior. Let's hope it was informative and able to provide you with all of the tools you need to achieve your goals whatever it may be.

The skills involved in analyzing people are varied and will depend on many different elements that are already ingrained in our subconscious mind. Whether you are using facial profiling, personality traits, or gestures, you will find that there is a powerful element of truth to being able to understand the people in your life.

Moreover, the skills you've learned in these pages can be used in just about every area of life.

How to Analyze People

Whether you're looking to land a new job and you want an edge on the competition, or you're shopping around for a new marriage mate, you will find many practical applications for the lessons you have learned here.

Still, to get the most out of analyzing people, remember the primary rule. You have to start by knowing who you are as a person. We are a compilation of our life experiences, culture, and environment. These can cause us to develop preconceived opinions about others that could literally interfere with our ability to understand and relate to others. Root those out as much as you can and identify those you can't. This will level the playing field and help you to become better at reading people.

Analyzing people can be a challenge, but it is a challenge worth taking. Through the pages of this book, you have learned how to read your own traits and understand the meaning of them. You have learned how to identify facial expressions, gestures, body language, and how to read the tone of voice and inflections to get to what a person is really saying.

We've talked about how to spot a lie when you hear it and a host of other useful skills along the way. Still, we have only scratched the surface as we went through these pages. If you feel you have learned something valuable and are curious to learn more, there are lots of websites on textbooks available that will unlock the secrets all humans try to hide. But for now, you are ready to go out and read the world you live in and as a result become a better person for it.

About the Author

Jessica Greiner is an author and a mother of two daughters. With a degree in Psychology, Jessica is passionate about helping people develop their inner emotional, psychic and sensual life. She believes that by understanding our brain and our emotions, why we do what we do, we are better equipped to deal with the various challenges we encounter in life.

Jessica writes books that are easy to understand and shares strategies that can be easily applied to everyone's day to day life. She has always been fascinated with the way people interact with others and the rest of the world. This interest has led her to the life of learning several factors affecting human interactions. Moreover, she continually works on expanding her knowledge by attending seminars and networking with other professionals.

When not writing, Jessica enjoys spending time horseback riding with her daughters or relaxing at the lake with her husband.